Mila gets her Super Ears

A story about how a little girl with hearing loss experiences listening, language and life.

Written by Ashley Machovec
Illustrated by Megan Jansen

For Mila, Katie, Fabio, Luca and Sofia

Thank you to my mom and dad for always helping me
make my dreams come to life.

A special shout out to Christine & Gregg Machovec, Jerry & Kim
McCaffrey, Katie & Fabio Petruzziello, Sergio Petruzziello,
Chris & Libby Rognier and Michael Bielik for your generous donations.
Without you, this book would not have been possible!

Do all things with kindness and compassion.
Together, we can change the world.

Hi!
I'm Mila!

I want to tell
you the story about
how I got my super ears!

1

It all started when I was a baby. When I was born, the doctors at the hospital told my mommy and daddy that I didn't pass my hearing screening.

Right away, my mommy and daddy made an appointment to see a special ear doctor. They wanted to make sure I could hear their voices, songs, doggies barking and cats meowing.

When you are a little baby, doctors can't test your ears like they can with big kids. Instead, they have to do a test called an ABR, or Auditory Brain Response.

The doctors stuck tiny stickers on my head and I fell asleep while they played loud and soft sounds. The doctors watched the machine to see which sounds my ears could hear, and which sounds they couldn't.

The doctors called my mommy and daddy to tell them that I had hearing loss, and gave me hearing aids to help me hear better. My mommy chose purple molds with sparkles...

I loved them SO much!

Now, I had a lot of work to do! I needed to practice hearing all of my new sounds. Mommy and Daddy found special therapists to help my ears hear with my hearing aids.

I started to work with a Teacher of the Deaf! This special teacher checks my hearing devices to make sure they work and teaches my family how to use and care for them.

She teaches my parents many different listening games so they can help me continue to build my listening skills when she isn't there.

I also started to work with a Speech Language Pathologist.

She helps me listen, communicate
with my friends and family
and say my sounds.

I see my therapists every week. I always have such a fun time with them. When they come to my house, my mommy, daddy and even my big brother join in!

Two years after I got my hearing aids, I started to notice it was getting harder to hear. I couldn't play my listening games as well as I used to.

At school, I couldn't hear my friends at snack time,

or when we played outside.

My Teacher of the Deaf, Speech Language Pathologist and family all noticed that I was not responding to sounds like I used to.

**When things were changing I felt a little bit nervous,
but I knew that my family and my therapists
were going to help me hear again.**

Mommy and Daddy took me to the audiologist. Now that I was a big kid, he could check my hearing in the listening booth! I put blocks in a bucket and stacked rings on a tower every time I heard a sound.

After my test, he sat down with my parents and told them that my hearing had dropped. That means that my ears could not hear sounds like they used to.

He told them not to worry though,
because there are cool

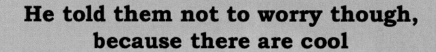

that I could get to help me hear again!
They are called cochlear implants!

Cochlear implants help
someone to hear when hearing
aids can't help them enough.

While I was waiting to get my cochlear implants, I still saw my therapists. It was important to keep practicing my listening, even when I couldn't hear everything like I used to.

I tried my best to practice my listening. I couldn't wait to get my cochlear implants. I was going to have my super ears in no time!

When the day finally came to get my super ears, Mommy, Daddy and I got into the car and went to the special ear doctor.

I started to feel a little nervous before the procedure to get my cochlear implants. I could tell my mommy and daddy were too, but our doctor came in and made us feel much better. I knew I was ready!

Everything went really well! Afterwards, I couldn't hear for a few weeks. It was a bit confusing not being able to hear anything for such a long time.

My mommy and daddy were the best though! They took such great care of me.

We had so much fun doing crafts and playing games together! They made sure I had everything I needed while I was waiting to hear again.

Before I knew it, it was activation day! Activation day is when you go to the audiologist to get your cochlear implants turned on.

She put on my processors and sent sounds to them.
"Beep!"...I HEARD THAT!
"Boop!"...I HEARD THAT TOO!

I was hearing again!
My super ears worked!
I noticed that they sounded a little
different from my hearing aids.

My cochlear implants communicate with my brain differently than my hearing aids. Everyone's voices sound so silly at first! Now I need to be trained to hear these new sounds with my super ears.

My Teacher of the Deaf and Speech Language Pathologist use a listening hoop to make my super ears super strong!

We play all of the same listening games as before, but I have to train my brain to listen as well as it did when I first got my hearing aids.

It can be difficult sometimes,
but I know they are going to help me
become the best listener I can be!

**My hearing journey is part of what makes me special.
I have super ears now!**

And I love them.

A note from Mila's parents:

Raising a child with hearing loss is a journey we never expected to embark on, but one that has opened up a beautiful new world to us. Along the way we've been so fortunate to have a wonderful team of professionals, specialists and friends to guide us, including Ashley and the amazing group at Listening Partners who provide so much love and support to Mila and our entire family. They have been our go-to resources for about a million questions and have shared many tools and strategies to help us support our fiercely determined and resilient little girl.

There aren't enough children's books that raise deaf awareness and explain hearing loss, hearing aids and cochlear implants in an upbeat and easy to understand way, so we were excited when Ashley said she wanted to write this book about Mila's journey. Mila inspires us every day and we hope her story serves as an inspiration to others. We hope this book provides other deaf or hard-of-hearing children with a character they can relate to and helps them to see that their hearing loss and "super ears" are part of what makes them so incredibly amazing and special.

We love this book and hope you do too.

The Petruzziello family

Ashley Machovec is an itinerant Teacher of the Deaf and Hard of Hearing in Purchase, NY. She received her masters degree from Teachers College at Columbia University where her interest in working with families and children with hearing loss grew into a true passion.

She noticed a lack of representation in children's books for the hearing loss community, and soon began on her new endeavor. This story was inspired by Mila's real life journey with hearing loss and her family's experiences going through the process of diagnosis, hearing aids, cochlear implantation and therapy. The hope for this book is to create a beautifully illustrated story that kids will love. It offers important information for the families to relate to and understand, and it will help your child celebrate their differences and their identity as a person with hearing loss.

Made in United States
North Haven, CT
17 February 2024

48822203R00022